PLAN @ 1:100

THINK @ **1:** ∞

PLAN @ 1:100

THINK @ 1: ∞

The Secret of Being Immortal

SANDEEP DESHMUKH

PARTRIDGE

A Penguin Company

Partridge books may be ordered through booksellers or by contacting:

Partridge India
Penguin Books India Pvt.Ltd
11, Community Centre, Panchsheel Park, New Delhi 110017
India
www.partridgepublishing.com
Phone: 000.800.10062.62

CONTENTS

SECTION ONE
The Secret of Being Immortal

SECTION TWO
Be Immortal

SECTION THREE
Go Beyond

This book is dedicated to my Parents and my Family.

SECTION ONE

THE SECRET OF BEING IMMORTAL

What is Plan @ 1:100 and Think@ 1: Infinity?

THE JOURNEY

One fine day as I was travelling in the local train to Churchgate I happened to meet Ashish Saxena, Rohit Dasgupta and Rakesh Chauhan. They were talking about how there are successful people in the world who have made themselves truly 'legends' of the world and that they will be remembered world over even long after their time has passed. Their ideas will be used time and again years after they themselves no longer exist. And how we (including me) will live a routine life and when we go, our identity, our ideas will fade away, we may be remembered by our very close next generation but that would probably be all. All the time Ashish, Rohit and Rakesh spoke about how they cannot be like the legends they talked about and wondered what the legends had done and they haven't. They had been discussing this for over a period in time and now the question was put to me. I began to wonder sometimes contemplating over it. Everyday somehow or the other the same topic came up, days passed by into weeks and weeks in months, we couldn't really come to any conclusion. We wondered—"What is the Secret of Being Immortal?"

I began reading books on leadership, self help books, anything and everything which could give me a simple answer to the simple question. Finally all my reading and thinking started to add up and I was now able to understand the basic guidelines or fundamentals required to being a success story 'The Legend'. Each book I read, each personal experience I analyzed gave me a unique insight into a new dimension I was studying, the more I read the more sure I was of the inherent secret of success. But since I dint know ARR (Ashish, Rohit and Rakesh) very well I realized it would be tough for me to explain to them what the legend did and they dint do (I would probably have to recite all the books I went through).

I started observing and studying them at near quarters. Ashish always carried his laptop and worked on it whenever time permitted. He used to be always in a hurry, catching the train at the last moment, cursing the train timetable and his boss for the early office hours. Rohit's constant companion was his cell phone, talking to his friends asking about their health, life—a social networking hub, I was told by Ashish and Rakesh that once every two months he takes glucose to keep up with his networking schedule (referring to a band aid patch on his hand) and Rakesh being an Investment Banker always talked about how much money is there to be made in the market, he always gave an impression that "here is one guy who thinks big" nonetheless he was amongst us financially very well off.

I wanted to give them an example which they would understand, I wondered about it for a few days, being from a technical background I started thinking in a more technical way, words started to flow into my mind, images started to take shape and now I was more or less convinced that I could explain to them in my own way what 'The legends' did and they dint do.

THE CHALLENGE

Next morning as I about to take my regular train to Chruchgate I was more eager to meet my newly found friends and start the journey of my insights into the question which bothered Ashish, Rohit and Rakesh.

"So, you mean you know the answer to our question?" they asked

"YES!" I said confidently.

"Ok, tell us about it."

"Well, you know guys, "The Legends", they really just Plan @ 1:100 and Think @ 1: Infinity." I said as a matter of fact.

"Sounds interesting, but you know, we are not from the building proposal department and neither are we Engineers, right? So, what exactly is Plan @ 1:100 and think at 1: Infinity?" Rohit voiced it out for all the others.

"Well simply put it is what Bill, Bell and Bappu did and we guys don't do." I said.

"Oh really, so who are these three guy's and what did they do? And do we know them?" Ashish questioned in amazement.

"O ya we know all of them, they are right in front of us, waiting to inspire us and we cherish all of them." I answered.

"This sounds interesting too, you mean to say we have the answer staring right in front of us and we don't even know about it. Come on convince me that I know about these three chaps' and that they plan @ 1:100 and think @ 1: infinity 'whatever that is' and I'll give you my laptop and you also get the new Windows 7 with it." Ashish challenged me.

"O ya I'll will give you my new Cell phone too." Rohit joined in.

"Well I can't give you the Bank, but I'll give you this crisp Rs1000 note." Rakesh said, as he flashed the note from his wallet.

I was very happy, I truly believed by the end of all this I will be having a new laptop, a cell phone and richer by Rs1000, not bad for convincing three guys on the train, right?

THE LEGENDS

"Once upon a time, a college dropout wrote a very 'BASIC' program which became the order of personal computers of the modern age"

Meet Mr. Bill Gates one of the richest and famous personalities of our times, is a legend by himself.

"Watson come here, I need you"

Meet Mr. Alexander Graham Bell the inventor of Telephone.

"An eye for an eye only makes the whole world Blind"

Meet Mr. Mohandas Gandhi, a Man who moved a nation by his ideas and the world by his vision.

Like a railway announcement for the arrival of next station I announced. This time around I managed to gain attention of few more of my fellow travelers, though impromptu.

It was as if everyone started to look out for them, they thought three more guys are going to join the already crowded train! After much deliberation, discussions and arguments all of us somehow came to a conclusion that Bill by way of computers, Bell by way of cell phones and Bappu by way of his image in the currency are always in front of us and that it depends on us whether we get inspired by them or not.

As the train reached Church gate station, I had accomplished one milestone in my challenge.

"Most of the legends or successful people are more often than not right in front of us, waiting for us to get inspired; we should open our mind to them, to get inspired or not is our own choice"

THE PROBLEM

The next day I saw Ashish running across the station as usual to catch the last train to Dadar that would take him to office on time. After much of huff and puff, Ashish put up a relieved face and uttered, "I just happened to save my day's salary". As the train moved on, we got into our regular chat,

Rakesh was eager to continue the discussions, where we had left it the other day and said, "So, the three b's definitely are legends in their own way, but they come from different fields of life, we come from different fields of life, then how can you blankly say "they plan at 1:100 and think at infinity" and we don't, what is it all about?" he questioned.

"Since they have been successful, it's very easy to say on the hind sight that they did certain things and that's why they are successful. Probably, these guys happened to be in the right place at the right time and the solution they gave worked, so they are successful." He added.

"Yes, I agree that it is very easy to say that a particular successful person did x, y, z things to be successful so we should also do the same. But that's not the point, what I mean to say is plan @ 1:100 and think @ 1: infinity has nothing to do with the specific solutions these guys got for their set of problems or goals. It's about how they thought about their problem or situation in their life. The legends knowingly or unknowing managed to align their thought process the Infinite way." I said.

Ashish was anxious; somehow I could see the words piling up in his mouth, which he finally blurted out.

"O yes! They never had to reach on time and face tyrants like my boss! Everyman's problem is different and only the person who goes through it understands best."

"So, you mean to say given a problem, these leaders would tend to think in a different way to find a solution compared to us." Rohit asked.

"Not really, most of the legends faced problems in different ways rather than just one way and found solutions for their problems by opening up their mind to infinite ways of thinking." I said.

"Let's say, in your personal or professional life you feel that there is no way ahead to your problems. There is no good solution to your problem; the option you are thinking is the only option available and even that option is not working because you think by adapting that option you will have so many other problems cropping up and so many more complications. You feel that it is a no win situation. Your mind is clogged with all these thoughts and you get entangled in these thoughts without getting any solution. In a way you start thinking, planning, working and moving in your own 'zone' or interpretations or your own analysis, perceptions and in turn confusing or diluting your thoughts which were 'good' or positive or workable in the first place. I would see this whole situation like a man thinking inside a room with walls on all four sides and the only solution he arrives at also hits a dead wall. It's like you are thinking in one wavelength or one scale." I said, as I went into an analytical mode.

"The leaders think in different scales, different wave lengths to achieve success." I was saying things which I had learnt through my research on legends; I was on a mission on a running train.

I was going to continue my thoughts when suddenly Ashish stood up from his seat completely ignoring what I had just spoken and said, "Come on; tell me what do I tell my boss once I reach office late? What would the so called leader's way of dealing with a simple problem like mine be?"

Amid spurts of laughter and giggle, Rakesh prompted, "O ya! May be we can analyze with Ashish's problem itself."

It was quiet obvious that Ashish was very angry about his situation and he would not listen to anyone now. He had already made up his mind that there is no way to deal with his problem and moreover he had concluded that his problems are because of someone else. As the train chugged along from one station to another all my discussion were leading nowhere and soon I realized that the only way to convince Ashish was to go to the Origins of Infinite Thinking and find him a solution.

INFINITE THINKING

Origins of Infinite Thinking

A week had passed by after my interaction with my train colleagues and in the mean time I had got an opportunity to further my research on the successful people, world leaders and legends. I soon realized that a leader would probably try to understand the problem first and then by thinking on the lines of Infinite thinking arrive at a solution which would be apt for the problem, not just for a short period of time but for an infinite period of time.

There were two quotes I read which caught my attention,

> **"Karmanye Vadhikaraste, Ma phaleshou kada chana,**
> **Ma Karma Phala Hetur Bhurmatey Sangostva Akarmani"**
> Bhagawat Gita

"Do your duty don't think of the fruits or failures in the way." And,

> **"Nobody can hurt me without my permission"** Mahatma Gandhi

I started analyzing Ashish's problem on similar lines. My first step was to understand the problem itself. My first reaction was that it's a common problem and many people may have gone through it and it's no big deal. But as I tried to analyze it further it gave me some very interesting insights into how to look at a problem and the probable way of finding a solution for it.

The Analysis: You often get late to office and because of that you either get a sound hearing from your boss or are penalized by a deduction in your salary at the end of the month. You get upset, angry, annoyed and try to find the best excuse to conclude that you dint deserve the penalty because you stayed late on so many other occasions and you leave late everyday and that you stay far away and that the HR or your senior is just taking his grudge against you or that the public transport is generally late and what can you do about it.

In the short term you may also find a quick fix solution to your problem—you may hire a cab, get up a little early and somehow manage to reach on time, just to save the salary next month. The situation may be tackled but did you ever sit back and think or write down the real reason for your situation. It could be just that you are plain lazy to get up on time to reach on time, or you may have to do few things at home before leaving like cooking, paying bills, dropping your kid to school, paying a visit to your ailing relative in hospital, doing another job to maintain the finances of the family. Though you might find a quick fix solution to your immediate problem, I wonder how long will the quick fix solutions last.

To really solve the problem you need to understand the problem itself. Whatever reason it may be, you need to understand it clearly. By defining the reason, your mind becomes clear of the choice you made, thus at the end of the month even if your salary gets deducted because of your irregularities, you are still in control, because it is the choice that you made, it maybe be by choosing personal life over professional life. By understanding the reason of choice you made, it is very easy to face any problem. If the problem was personal you could discuss it with your family members and get some feed back or you could also discuss your problem with your superiors in the office and make them aware of the personal difficulties you are facing. I am not saying that they will give you the leverage to come late, but yes they will now become aware of your situation. This is incidentally a positive action from your side to solve the problem. This method can be used to solve this problem amicably. As everyone has their own perception, the company would have been probably thinking that you were having a gala time coming late for your own good and that you care a damn about the company or them. By disclosing your difficulties to them you have, in essence, taken the first step to finding the solution to your problems. You would then, look at solving the problem together, which in effect gives altogether a different approach to the problem. The company might let you come late and ask you to put in some extra after hours. If workable they might ask you to work from home or else tell you to work for lesser hours on a reduced salary. They may still ask you to come early or tell you to quit and so on. The possibilities are endless, but the important thing for you to understand is that you are in charge or in control of the events that occur to you and people just react to your actions. If you got upset or angry because your salary got deducted it was because the company reacted to your action and now you are reacting to the reaction. The company saw your indiscipline as negative or detrimental to the goals and ideologies of the company and it just reacted to your actions. Your actions produced a negative action. Now imagine a reverse scenario, if you come on time every day, you will be measured as a disciplined employee and will create a positive atmosphere in the organization and the people surrounding you. Since you are expected to come on time you may not be rewarded for it but you will always get positive vibes from everyone. Alternately, if you have worked out a solution with your company such that you get flexible working hours, it would be in mutual agreement and hence produce only positive reactions.

So simply put,

Negative action produced Negative Reactions

Positive actions produce Positive Reactions.

So if we wish to get only positive reactions, we will have to do only positive actions. This is what my analysis had thought me about the situation and what I explained to Rohit, Rakesh and Ashish.

This philosophy is exactly what the legends know and practice in any situation or problem "Positive Actions to create Positive Reactions" and to get positive reactions from everyone they take into account everyone's thought process. This is where the origins of Infinite thinking come from.

Concept of Infinite Thinking

My analyses of Ashish's problem had helped me at least open up my colleagues mind set. Now they had started to believe that to find a solution to a problem you have understand the problem and to get positive reaction you have to do positive actions. But they were not able to understand how to get positive reactions from everyone.

"But is it really possible to capture thought processes of many people into your actions?" Rakesh enquired.

"Well practically no, but yes you can capture the spirit of humanity in your thought process, your actions and achieve the result you want. The leaders capture the spirit of humanity in their thinking; and in essence they align their thought process to the principles of infinite thinking" I said.

"What the hell are you talking about 'Spirit of Humanity'? I find this statement too easy to say in an ideal scenario, but when the question of Roti (Food), Kappda (Clothing) and Makkan (Shelter) comes into picture, the "Spirit of Humanity" is the first to disappear in thin air." mocked Rohit blowing air as if he was smoking a cigar.

Hearing this, everybody started laughing, even few of the commuters who were listening to our conversation put on broad smiling faces, as if all seemed to agree with Rohit. It was true, I couldn't less disagree, but that's exactly what I wanted to explain to them. The basic difference between the thought process of leaders and commoners like us!

"Have you heard of the Maslow's Law?" I roared, being a bit agitated by all the mocking.

Somehow in tandem a question propped up from as many as about 20 people in the compartment, "What Law!"

I didn't realize so many were really listening to our conversation. Baffled I continued "Maslow's law talks about basic hierarchy of needs of mankind, levels and stages of attainments. It talks about how if only our primary needs are satisfied then we start to think of the next level of our requirements. In other words the basic roti, kappda and makkhan come from these very basic requirements of humankind.

"Wow I didn't know somebody made a law out of our basic needs!" Rakesh said in amazement.

"Well Maslow's did and he too comes in my list of Infinite thinkers, his ideas are accepted world over and have lasted for many years." I asserted.

"Well then, are you proving through this 'Law' that everyone think from their basic requirements perspective? If so, then how can a leader or legend think any differently? Do you mean legends don't have these basic requirements?" Rohit said in a very sarcastic way winking at Ashish and Rakesh at the same time.

"Not at all, every human has these basic requirements to fulfill and the legends are no exception to that" I admitted, "but that's where the similarity between them and commoners like us end"

"What do you mean?" the inquisitiveness of the listeners was growing. I could sense it, it was on their faces. They wanted to know what separates the legends from the commoners.

I started looking up the rack where I had kept my office bag. Before I knew it, few people had given it to me. I started searching for some of my sketches I was working on when I had started this quest. Soon enough I found those in the back of my bag.

"Look at this diagram, the first one is the Maslow's law. Clearly defined in a triangular sketch talking about the basic needs of mankind and how only after achieving one stage, a person really goes to the next stage of thinking." I said going into a complete presentation mode, holding the sketches high and resting my back on the window.

Balancing myself in the fast moving train, I pulled up another sketch and said, "the legends on the other hand see this sketch as seen in sketch '2'. They tend to align their thought process with all the factors listed in Maslow's law. Each of their decision is based such that, each of the given requirements is considered. So in effect they capture the spirit of humanity in anything they set out to achieve." I said as I compared the two charts.

The charts which I had sketched started circulating in the compartment, as I continued my presentation.

"The triangle in essence gives the needs of Humans in a nut shell, in a way capturing the spirit of humanity in it, the leaders tend to capture the spirit of humanity in their thought process, that's were their thought process differs from our thought process." Saying this I realized that it was an excellent time to talk about the concept of Infinite thinking.

"If our intentions are such that they are based on principles that take into account everyone's thought process or ideologies there won't be any negative reaction to our actions. Our actions will only create positive reactions, like the waves of the ocean, they all go in one direction, the ones which go in the opposite direction create lot of dynamic reactions but last only for a limited time. If the thought process is based on something timeless, the thoughts will also be timeless; if it is based on the concept of serving everyone it will receive maximum positive reaction like the waves of the ocean. The legends think on the "Principles of timelessness"

As I continued my discussion Ashish enquired, "Positive actions create Positive reaction seems fine, but what do you mean by "thought process should be timeless" what is this philosophy?"

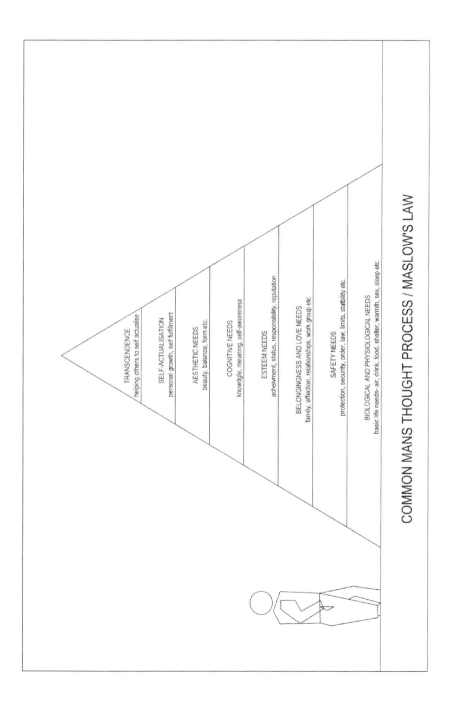

COMMON MANS THOUGHT PROCESS / MASLOW'S LAW

TRANSCENDENCE
helping others to self actualise

SELF-ACTUALISATION
personal growth, self fulfillment

AESTHETIC NEEDS
beauty, balance, form etc.

COGNITIVE NEEDS
knowdgle, meaning, self-awareness

ESTEEM NEEDS
achievment, status, responsibility, reputation

BELONGINGNESS AND LOVE NEEDS
family, affection, relationships, work group etc.

SAFETY NEEDS
protection, security, order, law, limits, statbility etc.

BIOLOGICAL AND PHYSIOLOGICAL NEEDS
basic life needs- air, drink, food, shelter, warmth, sex, sleep etc.

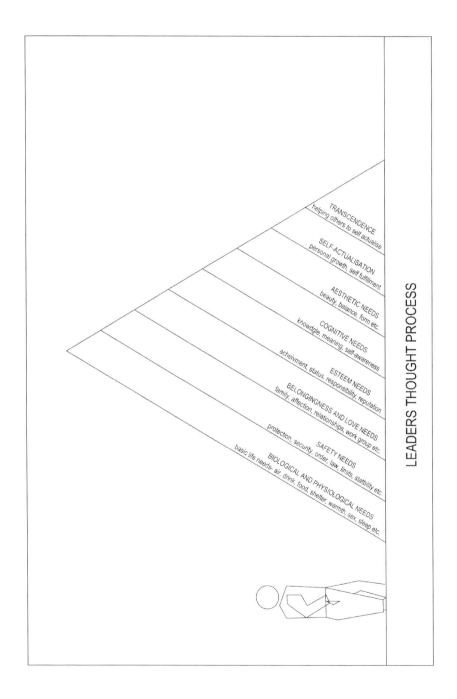

LEADERS THOUGHT PROCESS

TRANSCENDENCE
helping others to self actualise

SELF-ACTUALISATION
personal growth, self fulfillment

AESTHETIC NEEDS
beauty, balance, form etc.

COGNITIVE NEEDS
knowdgie, meaning, self-awareness

ESTEEM NEEDS
acheivment, status, responsibility, reputation

BELONGINGNESS AND LOVE NEEDS
family, affection, relationships, work group etc.

SAFETY NEEDS
protection, security, order, law, limits, slatbility etc.

BIOLOGICAL AND PHYSIOLOGICAL NEEDS
basic life needs- air, drink, food, shelter, warmth, sex, sleep etc.

Principles of Infinite Thinking

"A man generally thinks in a particular scale; the scale of thinking is based on his perceptions and his basic characteristics. When he sets out to achieve anything in this world, he plans according to his ability and capacity and after achieving his goal his idea becomes a success. But how long his idea or success will last depends on whether he has aligned his thought process to something which has stood the test of time." I said.

Everyone in the compartment by now was as eager as Ashish was. Everyone wanted to know, what had stood the test of time? Somehow my belief was that everybody already knew the answer and that it had to come from them. I started cross questioning.

"What has lasted the test of time? What is it that lasted for a long time and is still applicable or can be adapted? Which are the thoughts that have lasted for a longer period of time? What are the principles of being successful since ages? What are the types of people who are remembered time and again? Is there anything which is Infinite?"

After a brief period of interaction with my fellow passengers I started getting some brilliant suggestions. One prompted 'Nature', some one out in the middle said 'God', I heard someone say 'Space', and there were others who said 'Innovation and Discoveries', some said 'Change' while others talked about the 'Characteristics and Qualities' of Legends which has stood the test of time.

Each answer had something timeless in it.

Mother Nature: She has lasted the test of time and is still there, if we adopt her way of things and respect her we will be thinking timeless. If we imbibe her principles in our thought process we will be thinking like the waves of the ocean, we will be thinking @ 1:∞.

Concept of GOD: He has been there since civilization erupted and still people believe in god. The paths of god are many, with many interpretations of god. But it essentially talks about a superior power. Believing in the concept of GOD or superior being or belief in belief itself is like thinking like the waves of the ocean thinking @ 1:∞.

Teachings of God: These religious texts like the Bhagwat Gita, the Bible, and the Kuran have been there since ages and have stood the test of time. Following the principles laid down for the people by these religious books is like the waves of the ocean, it's like thinking 1:∞.

Space: Space is nothing but infinity itself, it shows that infinity exists.

Characteristics of people thinking 1:∞: Some universal human qualities that have stood the test of time are Empathy, Honesty, Integrity, Courage, Consistency, Love, Passion, Compassion, Sacrifice, Vision, Curiosity, Discipline, Strategic Thinking, Devotion, and Modesty. Most of the Legends we know have some of these qualities which form the basis of thinking @ 1:∞.

Innovations and Discoveries: Something's which have always stood the test of time for longer periods of time are Innovations and Discoveries.

Change: Change is the only constant in thinking 1:∞. The idea should be adaptable to the time it is set in and the time it will be set in future.

The points mentioned above are things we people cherish every day and when they are disturbed we get disturbed. Aligning our thoughts to these fundamentals will ensure timelessness of our thoughts that's the spirit of thinking @ 1:∞.

As the train moved along one of the commuters enquired, "So, you mean to say each of the legends has in one way or the other used these principles to achieve what they achieved."

"Yes, but they also believed that to achieve anything you should know what you want to achieve, set a goal for yourself, align it to the principles of infinity. The road to infinite thinking is simple; success is assured if you follow the path. The choice of goal could be personal or professional but aligning it to the principles of infinity is something special, it's about going beyond of just being successful, it ensures immortality to your success." I said, adding that the Legends not just thought at 1: Infinity but to reach their goal they also planned at 1:100, the way they understood, adapted and delivered it.

"So how do you think at infinity and plan at 100?" I knew this question would prop up, and eventually it did, from everyone who was listening to me.

PLAN @ 1:100 THINK @ 1: INFINITY

To define thinking at infinity in a single line is in a way limiting its boundless extent of its reach and potential, still to put it a nut shell

"Infinite thinking is a thinking process which shows you a 'way' to open your mind to infinite thinking, which you thought never existed and in the process ensuring that your ideas last infinitely"

"Planning at 1:100 idea, is based on the thought process that whatever you think at infinity has to be adaptable, applicable and usable by everybody in general"

Infinite thinking sets you thinking in the fourth dimension "Time"

To understand and follow Plan@1:100 Think @ 1: Infinity thinking process you need to first understand what is,

1. Perceptions and Scales.
2. Prerequisites.
3. Learning to Manage your Thoughts.
4. And Finally, Plan @ 1:100, Think @ 1:∞

The legends have understood the concepts above and achieved success in whatever they pursued and made it last for infinite period of time.

Examples of Legends in different fields of life,

M. K. Gandhi: He wanted to wipe every tear from every eye, he stood up for a belief that all human beings are creations of the same god and all are equal. He stood up for the spirit of Humanity; his thought process was based on thinking at infinity. He planned at 1:100 so that people could use his ideas and implement them easily. He protested in a non-violent way, he tried to keep everyone together and developed love, affection and respect among all his freedom fighters.

Even today Gandhi's methods are considered as the best methods of protest, he is truly the father of the Nation, and will be remembered forever.

Abraham Lincoln: His aim was to preserve the union of America and abolish slavery. He stood up for the spirit of humanity and strived towards it. He fought for the liberty of humanity from slavery, his thought process was aligned to the principles of infinity; success was just around the corner.

Jamsetji Tata: A pioneer, a visionary, a seer-perhaps these adjectives are not enough to describe a man of such extraordinary caliber and stature who has secured a strong foothold in the map of industrial nations of the world. The creative forces of his genius were harnessed to cater to the development of his own land and his dream arising out of intense love of humanity.

Mother Teresa: Dedicated to serving poor people, she believed in serving the god in people.

Bill Gates: Applied his skills to innovations and business management and achieved tremendous success. He is now turned into a philanthropist, serving humanity in his own way.

Albert Einstein: Developed General theory of relativity affecting a revolution in physics.

Galileo: Responsible for the birth of modern science.

I believe that by aligning our thought process to the principles of infinite thinking we can achieve,

- Personal successes
- Professional success.
- Social success.
- Successful contribution to the world which will last infinitely.

All of the above together by just doing what we have been doing!

So simply put, if we don't align our thought process to the principles of infinite thinking our thought process don't last long enough and fade away much before we fade away and as long as we apply these principles in our lives our success is guaranteed over a longer period of time, ensuing immortality.

Coming back to my discussions with my fellow passengers, over the next following several days we discussed the principles of infinite thinking and the steps required to be taken to plan @ 1:100 at great lengths. By now, Ashish had started reading these books and was now a proactive part of the dialogues between us. He was now the first person to catch the train, and I hardly found him getting late for office. He had also started adding to the discussions and now I had one person agreeing to my view points and two still not completely convinced but open to the thought process of infinite thinking. This as per me was the second milestone of success for the challenge.

"Do not believe in anything simply because you have heard it. Do not believe in anything simply because it is spoken and rumored by many. Do not believe in anything simply because it is found written in your religious books. Do not believe in anything merely on the authority of your teachers and elders. Do not believe in traditions because they have been handed down for many generations. But after observation and analysis, when you find that anything agrees with reason and is conducive to the good and benefit of one and all, then accept it and live up to it."—Buddha

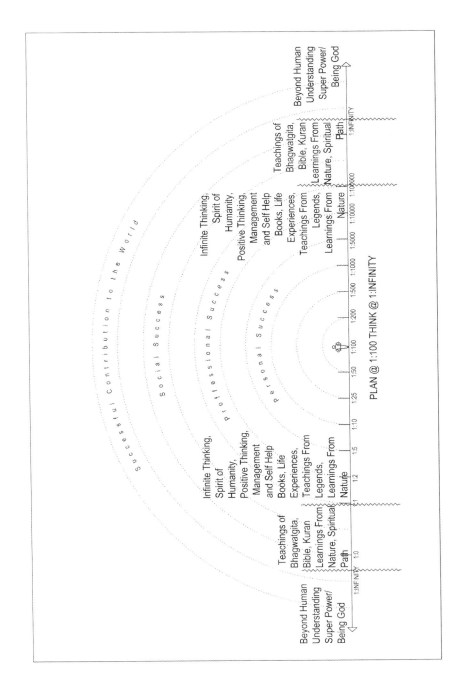

Successful Contribution to the World

Social Success

Proffesional Success

Personal Success

Infinite Thinking,
Spirit of
Humanity,
Positive Thinking,
Management
and Self Help
Books, Life
Experiences,
Teachings From
Legends,
Learnings From
Nature

Teachings of
Bhagwatgita,
Bible, Kuran
Learnings From
Nature, Spiritual
Path

Beyond Human
Understanding
Super Power/
Being God

1:INFINITY   1:100000   1:10000   1:5000   1:1000   1:500   1:200   1:100   1:50   1:25   1:10   1:5   1:2   1:1   1:INFINITY

PLAN @ 1:100 THINK @ 1:INFINITY

Infinite Thinking,
Spirit of
Humanity,
Positive Thinking,
Management
and Self Help
Books, Life
Experiences,
Teachings From
Legends,
Learnings From
Nature

Teachings of
Bhagwatgita,
Bible, Kuran
Learnings From
Nature, Spiritual
Path

Beyond Human
Understanding
Super Power/
Being God

SECTION TWO

BE IMMORTAL

How to Plan @ 1:100 and Think@ 1: Infinity

PERCEPTIONS AND SCALES

The Vision

Rakesh was ecstatic; he couldn't believe what he was reading. The Business Times read, 'Mount Everest Inc. taken over by Eagle Vision'. Rakesh went on to explain that the market capitalization of ME Inc. was 40 Billion and that of Eagle Vision was one billion on the positive side. He had no idea how such a thing could happen. But it did. The peak of Mount Everest was reached by some company who had vision. Soon enough, Rakesh's face went low, he frantically tried to call his broker but what he heard on the other side disappointed him further. Soon we realized Rakesh had the knowledge about Eagle vision's growth plans and strategies but he could not imagine that such a growth story was ever possible. It was beyond his scale to think of such a possibility. He had lost a golden opportunity to make a hell lot of money. He talked about how he had a dream of building a home for himself on his ancestral property and that this money could have helped him achieve his dream home.

Big Fish Small Fish

To understand where we stand with respect to the world and our scale of thinking is not easy. For example, we may feel like a big fish in a small pond or a small fish in the sea. It s all relative, perceptions of people are developed over the years starting from their formative years where they see, interact with people and start developing their own perceptions of the world. Our perceptions actually define what scale we can think. Any situation we face in life is tackled based on these perceptions. What we perceive is what we feel is right and we find it hard to break away from those perceptions. This perception is what gets defined as our scale of thinking. This scale of thinking remains constant until our experiences or knowledge changes, which in turn changes our scale of thinking. Everyone has a set scale of thinking; this scale can be defined as the general scale an individual thinks in, I say a scale of 1:100, is a general scale. Each individual has a different scale of thinking and that base thinking of that person is his scale of thinking. Every person comes from a different background, goes through different life experiences, have different beliefs, value systems, financial conditions and neighborhoods. Each of these aspects moulds a person into an individual who thinks and acts differently from the other. Each individual's perceptions are unique to him and hence the individual reacts differently to a situation than some other person facing the same situation.

Dream House

Rakesh's dream home vision had struck a chord in me. I wanted to know more about his vision, so I asked him "Tell me more about this dream home vision of yours"

Rakesh got excited he said, "I have my ancestral property in lonavala on the edge of a mountain cliff and want to build a house there."

"So what's stopping you from achieving your goal, I am sure you have enough kitties in your bag" I gestured with my fingers crossed.

"Not really, if I have to peruse this dream of mine I may not be able to buy the sedan I am eyeing to buy now. I am really confused. I don't know where to start or what to do." Rakesh sounded dejected.

"I don't know if I have the budget to build the house and still buy the sedan." He cribbed.

I began probing further, I asked many questions to Rakesh just to find out if he was clear about his vision of the dream home he intended to build and always dreamt of.

"What is the purpose of the bungalow? Is it a 1st home 2nd or 3rd one? Is it a weekend gateway? Is it a Residence plus business destination? How much do you want to build? What is the look you want for your house? Are you looking at a swimming pool a lawn tennis court? Have you allocated any funds for it?"

It was soon very clear to me that most of the questions remained unanswered and I had to really take them out from him. He was not clear what he really wanted. It was his dream house and he was still dreaming about it and had not worked on his dream to make it into his vision. After further probing he said that if there are so many things which need to be done to achieve his dream home, then he would rather hire a consultant to do the job for him as he cannot visualize or think about so many things before hand.

The Consultant

He may be an expert a particular field, a guru or your mentor. He may give you few suggestions and try to get the correct requirement from you. But after this exercise he will more or less know what you are looking for. When your consultant knows your goal, he puts on his thinking cap, he looks at your goal 'dream home' in a very professional way. Your dream house is a goal for a professional. He starts visualizing and conceptualizing your dream home. He starts with a basic concept of the entire scheme of things 'Your Dream Home' is now a concept for him, which in true sense is 1: Infinity. Over a period of time he discusses your dream home and now you are beginning to see your dream home turning into a real home. He starts showing you plans in 1:100 so that you understand what your building is, how the spaces are. He makes views, sketches, draws plans at varied scales to explain each and every aspect of the building.

As the building begins to take shape on the drawing board you realize because of time, money and space constraints your dream home is very close to your dream but not exactly 100% to what you dreamt off—the dream home is getting adapted to the real world. Coming back, the consultant gives you the following plans,

1. Concept plan @ (1:infinity)
2. Location plan @ 1:10000
3. A layout plan @ 1:1000
4. A site plan @ 1:500

5. A floor plan @ 1:100
6. Interior plans @ 1:50
7. Details @ 1:20, 1:5, 1:2 & 1:1

He has drawn plans from 1: infinity to 1:1 to give you your DREAM HOME the way you want it, and if you follow the plans you will get what you wanted for sure. Also one of the most important aspect about these drawings is most of the drawings which are given to you are in 1:100 scale, a scale best understood by many. The other scales are either related more to construction engineers to construct or for municipal approvals. The concept, what he gave you, was the selling/ or buying point for you, in effect meaning if the goal is clear to you, you will go for it. The consultant plans @ 1:100, but thinks @ 1:∞

This example is just one method of how you would achieve things what you want to achieve and how things are done in a professional manner.

The consultants example made us all realize that, we really have to think and plan in all scales, if we want to achieve our dream target. As Rakesh's lack of imagination had failed him to capitalize on his in-depth knowledge of the capital market, I remembered one of Albert Einstein's quotes I had read,

> **"Imagination is more important than knowledge"**—Albert Einstein

The Query

"You mean to say even the legends take help of consultants/ mentors to achieve their goal." Ashish said.

"In fact legends will leave no stone unturned to achieve their goal, consultant or no consultant." I said

"But how can we open our mind to different ways of thinking or think in different scales without a consultant/ mentor, it's not going to be cheap hiring consultants for every small thing you know." Rohit enquired.

"Consultant is just one mode to achieve success in established areas, most of the planning and thinking has to stem out from within us, the consultant just guides us towards the goal, he can only get us close to our goal, only we know our goal best. We need to first understand where we are (our perceptions/ scale of thinking), where we want to go (goal) and learn to think in different scales to help us achieve our goal" I said adding that to really open our mind to thinking at infinity we have to join the nine dots and define our scale of thinking.

The Nine Dots and You

It is basically a puzzle of nine dots and you have to join them in four continuous lines, as hard as you can try to, you will never really be able to join these nine dots in four continues straight line, unless you see beyond the boundary, the nine dots have created. The invincible boundary which is created by the dots is called the boundary of perception. Once you understand your limitation, you can then identify that the boundary exists and then cross beyond it. Figure "A" shows you that the boundary exists and Figure "B" tells you to think beyond perception. Once you believe there are possibilities beyond your thinking, it gets much easier.

Thinking at infinity is all about joining those dots by going beyond the boundaries of thinking limitation. The example of nine dots defines your perception of the situation and you imaginary boundary of thinking or thinking limitation.

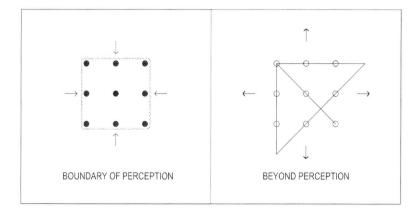

BOUNDARY OF PERCEPTION   BEYOND PERCEPTION

Define Your Scale

Once you know about your perceptions it will be easy to search for different scales of thinking. It could be 1:200 or 1:50 or any other scale (which is nothing but thinking in a different perspective or scale).

Your failures teach you a lot in your life. In your everyday life, you or your loved one may come across many situations, like having to clear an examination or interview to get into higher college or to get promoted, or it could be a business deal you wanted to clinch. You may have put in your best efforts into it to be successful. You may be sure that you would be successful. But in spite of your best efforts you may not be successful in achieving what you set out to achieve. You may have failed in your attempt to clear the hurdle. It's like; you are staring at a wall, with the only door to success, shut on your face. You had worked for it, there were others like you who had tried to go through that door of success, and some of them did manage to go through. You were the 'others' who got left out. The 'door of opportunity' which was open some time ago is now closed, it may open after some time, but it is shut for now. Whatever you do, you cannot change the past. There is no point pondering over the past, the only thing you can take along from your failure is the rich experience of failure, because these failures will be the stepping stones to your success later in life. Failures' are life's biggest learning experiences, if you choose them to be and they can help you in improving yourself. It teaches you in the crudest form that a perception exits and that your perceptions alone will not guarantee success in your actions and that it is important to learn and understand different scales of thinking to be successful.

To help you visualize your situation in different scales, consider a situation where in a wall is made spanning across the world, dividing it into two parts. You have to go from one side to the other side of the world to achieve your goal. The dividing wall has few doors in it of different sizes and they remain open only for a limited period of time and allow only a few people to pass through it. Each door leads you into a unique world of opportunity on the other side. The doors have name plates which tell exactly where it would lead you too. For example the door name plates read like the following;

- Entry to MBA course in IIT.

- Muti-million dollar business deal of Microsoft.
- Promotion to the CEO post.

There are many other doors leading you to different places of success, but all these doors are scattered throughout the length of the wall. From the place where you stand you can only see few doors. Look at figure "1", from the place where you stand you can see an endless wall with some doors to go to the other side. Since you have been unsuccessful in your efforts you can see that the door you were trying to enter has closed. There are few people who have crossed over to the other side. It looks like a hopeless situation to you as the door may not open again and you are left stranded with few others like you. You either have to wait for the door to open or look at another option. If you look carefully, you will also see a small opening in the wall, which few people have used to go to the other side. This opening depicts that, there still exits options even in the scale you are thinking, it is just a question of applying your mind to it.

Now look at figure "2", at a broader scale of thinking, you will note that you can see few more doors to go to the other side. You can see more opportunity. Notice the lost opportunity door, the limited opening door, the untried lost opportunity and the bigger mass opening door. Suddenly you will realize that, there exits many more options at this scale. It was just a question of thinking at higher scales. In effect your failures have now thrown in many more options and opportunities you may have missed earlier. Your failures are teaching you to think at different scales and helping you take steps towards infinite ways of thinking.

Figure "3" depicts thinking at much higher scales, it talks about different openings of different sizes and shapes and varied number of people on the other side of each opening. There are also a lot of people on the side where you used to be. But since you have moved on to newer scales, new ways of thinking, you are seeing new possibilities. Now you have truly opened the doors to opportunities and options which you thought never existed, but they have now started giving you new hope, new direction and a new meaning to your life. Also, you are now able to see that beyond each door there are different number of people, this information helps you identify areas where competitions are less in short term and shortage in service to people if you think @ 1: infinity.

There are also areas which don't have the wall as a barrier and there are even no people on the other side. The road to that end looks quite far from your present location but it looks like the best option as there is no competition as well. Thinking on a much higher scale/level gives you options which are sometimes untouched by many.

Define your scale to learn about higher and lower scales in life.

"If the doors of perception were cleansed everything would appear to man as it is, infinite"—William Blake.

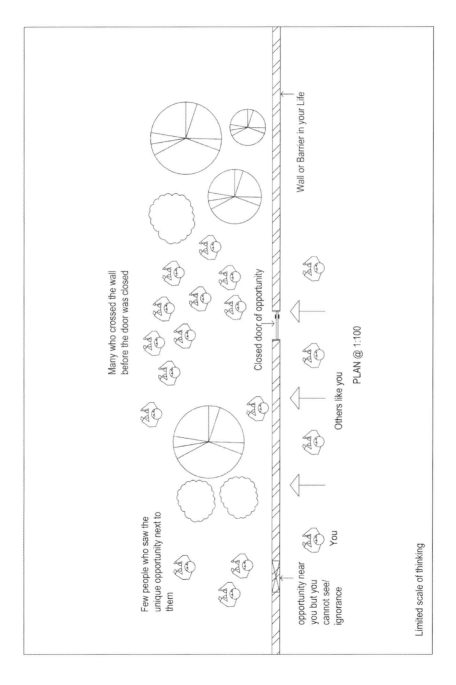

Many who crossed the wall
before the door was closed

Few people who saw the
unique opportunity next to
them

opportunity near
you but you
cannot see/
ignorance

You

Closed door of opportunity

Others like you

Wall or Barrier in your Life

PLAN @ 1:100

Limited scale of thinking

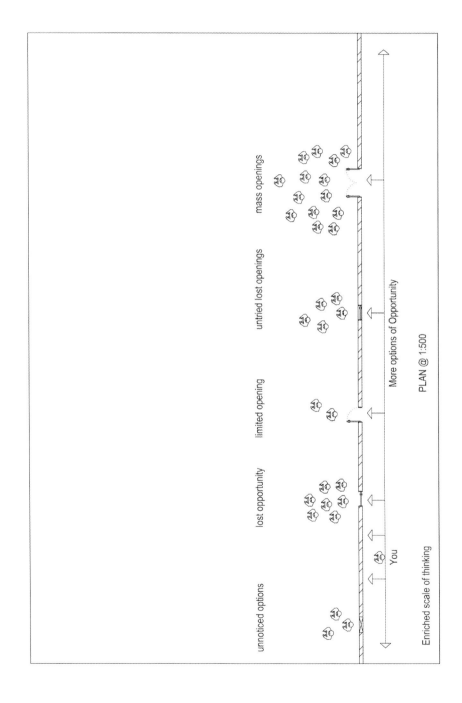

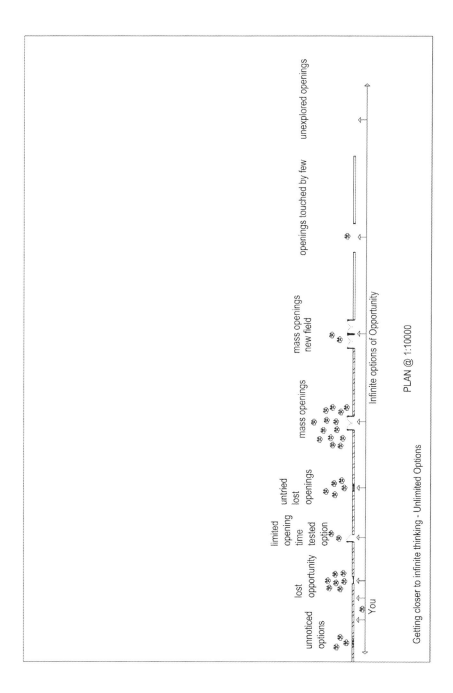

Getting closer to infinite thinking - Unlimited Options

PLAN @ 1:10000

Infinite options of Opportunity

unnoticed options

lost opportunity

You

limited opening time tested option

untried lost openings

mass openings

mass openings new field

openings touched by few

unexplored openings

37

Open up your Mind

There will always be a question on how to train our mind to think differently from the way we have been thinking.

Since birth we are conditioned to certain way of living and interacting with the world around us and as such our thinking gets moulded to a particular way of thinking. Since this becomes the backbone of our thinking, it is important to first define our perception and our scale of thinking. Once we are able to clearly define our scale (1:100) of thinking, our attitude and essential characteristics will guide us through our journey to opening our mind to infinite thinking. Since we are accustomed to a particular way of thinking first we have to move away from it, this can be done from any of the following ways. Each guide will help you attain a new scale in your thinking. You can follow one or all of the points to achieve unimaginable thought process for different scales of thinking.

- Age groups, by discussing with different age groups, you get different perspectives of people living in different scales of thinking, you can ask a 10,20,30,40,50,60,70 . . . year old what they feel about your problems and ask for their solutions to it, consider their ideas.
- Religion: ask people of different religion to get different perspectives and view point.
- Ask/ consult an expert/ professional in that field
- Educate yourself in the field of your aim.
- Solve your problem by sketching it! Sometimes visuals give ideas no teaching can.
- Think backwards, flip the problem upside down.
- Think randomly
- Think how a blind man travels in a local train.
- Read books, watch movies, ads; these are hot beds of creativity.
- Learn from nature get inspired from it, how she has designed everything for us.
- Think with constraints and then think totally without them.

The sky is the limit to open your mind to thinking at different scales. It all depends whether you have the right attitude and essential characteristic to do it.

By now Ashish, Rakesh and Rohit's understanding about perceptions and scales had begun to make an impact on their thinking. Rakesh stated that Eagle vision's vision was bigger than Mount Everest heights and that's why it could take over a giant 40 times bigger than itself.

As I saw Rakesh getting more convinced about infinite thinking, I felt yet another milestone achieved towards my challenge,

"Thinking Big is not so important; having a clear vision is absolute" —Unknown

"If you wish to advance into infinite, explore the finite in all directions"— Johann Wolfgang Von Goethe.

THE PREREQUISITES

AB+

For the past few days we had not seen Rohit in the train. So when he did join us one day in our regular train journey, we were keen to know what the reason for his disappearance was. We came to know that someone from his family had met with an accident and that he had been with that relative for the past few days.

"The Merc. It rammed into my uncles bike throwing him 10mts across the street. He had lost lot of blood. The hospital could not arrange for his type of blood group AB+ and time was running out, that's when my aunty called me to help her." Rohit said.

We sympathized with Rohit, Rakesh enquired" If the hospital could not help her, how could you."

"Actually, even I dint know how I could help, I tried calling few of my friends in the blood donation camp and they said they would help, within a couple of hours they had managed to arrange for donors of AB+ blood group. I don't know how I can ever thank them; I am indebted and grateful to them: they saved my uncles life." We could see tears in his eyes as he said it softly.

We become curious, "How did you know these doctors? It would be really good to know them, especially in an emergency." Ashish asked.

"I happened to meet them in the blood donation camp where I go to donate blood."

He said it with that simplicity, my memory took me back to the patch I had noticed on Rohit's hand few months back, the story added up. His good deeds were paying him back. I felt Rohit already had the prerequisites we were discussing when he was not around.

I thought "AB+ is Always Be Positive in your actions it will help you and others some way or the other.

"The great gift of human beings is that we have the power of empathy, we can all sense a mysterious connection to each other"—Meryl Streep

Look Within

There have been so many instances and events in our history giving us rich insights into the people who rose to fame, did what they did to achieve something considered unachievable by many at that time. These men have shown true spirit of mankind displaying qualities like honesty, integrity, courage, consistency, compassion, charity, sacrifice, innovation, vision, curiosity, discipline, focus, etc. Each of these qualities have stood the test of time. But the biggest quality in all these men was that they had a "Proactive Positive Attitude' towards their goal. I call this the first baby step towards your goal.

The Baby is Born

A child takes his first steps by just being positive. After falling innumerable times he eventually learns to crawl and then walk, jump and eventually run. He shows unmatched determination, courage, innovation, curiosity to achieve his goal. If a baby requires so many qualities just to walk, don't you think in life we have so many big challenges yet we hardly use any of these inherited qualities?

If the baby had thought negatively in the first place he would never be able to walk for the rest of his life, just by thinking positively and building on failures he achieves his goal. My personal belief is all men are god gifted to have an open mind or rather have the ability to think in all scales.

Children up to the age of 5 years tend to learn almost anything quickly, since they are not still moulded into any way of thinking they can accept any concept and learn from it. As they grow older they develop their perceptions about the world around and with time this becomes their scale of thinking and they generally start to think in that scale.

As the baby learns from his surrounding to walk and run from his surroundings, he also learns about the way we behave, talk, love, hate, fight, have religious beliefs, understand money etc. These learning's and understandings form the foundations of his perceptions later in life and these will govern the way he thinks in life and also at what scale he can keep his mind open.

The example of baby teaches us to have a proactive positive attitude in life. Also since the foundation of perception are formed early in life, it is of utmost importance that the thought process of thinking in 1: Infinity is imbibed early in life into each and every person.

Earlier we looked at perceptions and scales. Now we will try to analyze another situation to understand how a person would act or react to a situation based on his perceptions, scale and characteristics and finally how each ones thinking generates different ideas or solutions to the same problem.

The Trench

In my discussions with Ashish, Rakesh and Rohit we had discussed about how to find a solution to any problem. We had taken three different examples of a trench, wherein in each example the patron had to cross the trench to reach to the other side considering the other side had better prospects for success.

- A. Trench 5 feet wide 6 inches deep
- B. Trench 5 feet wide 5 feet deep
- C. Trench 5 feet wide 1000 feet deep.

For the first problem our solution was just to jump over and go.

For the second problem we started to think about an alternative, as we had a doubt whether we will be able to cross it or not but eventually all of us decided to risk it and jump.

For option "C" we decided it is not worth taking the risk and started to think about an alternate solution for it. We also concluded that most of the people would not risk it and definitely think about searching for an option for it.

We also tried to test the problem with the principles of Infinite Thinking. We took the example and tried to probe the problem further and eventually came up with some surprising solutions which are listed in the following pages, but before you flip to those pages, consider that if you had to face problem, What would be your solution to the problem? Would you jump and cross over or think about an alternative? What are the options you came up with? Did you think more options were possible? What was the basis of your solution to the problem? It would be helpful for you to understand your scale of thinking if you can answer these questions before you go further.

Now let us go to the following sketches and study all the options. Each option shown has an inherent aim, i.e., to cross over to the other side, but the method adopted is different in each case. Every solution has a different way of thinking and it is based on different perceptions, scale of thinking which in turn is governed by the life experiences and characteristics. Each path will give its fruits and failures. Which path you take is your decision, it may or may not benefit you in the short or medium term but if your actions are aligned to the principles of infinite thinking then you are assured that the thought process you have considered will last forever.

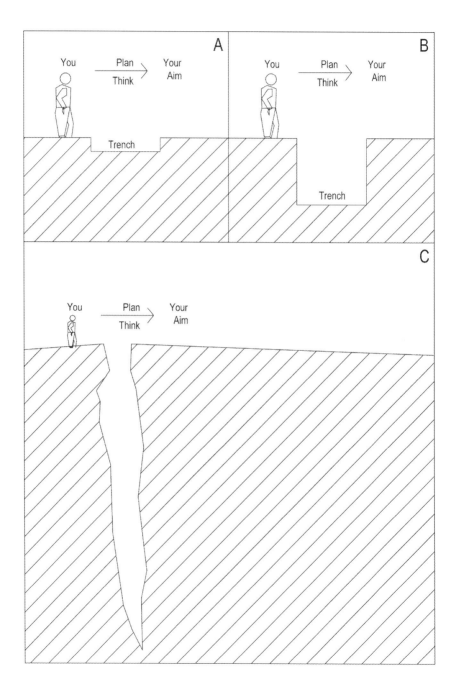

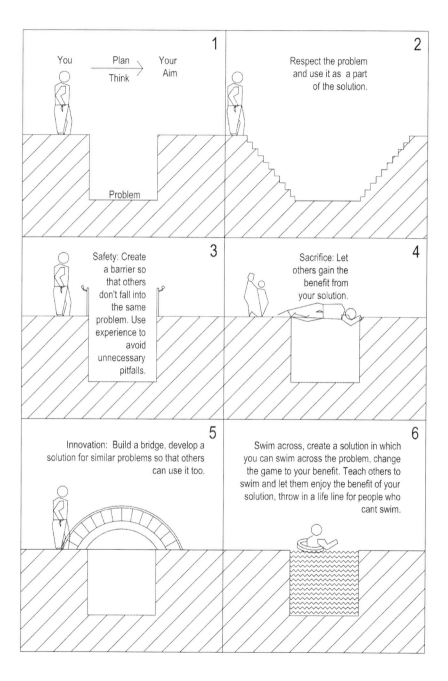

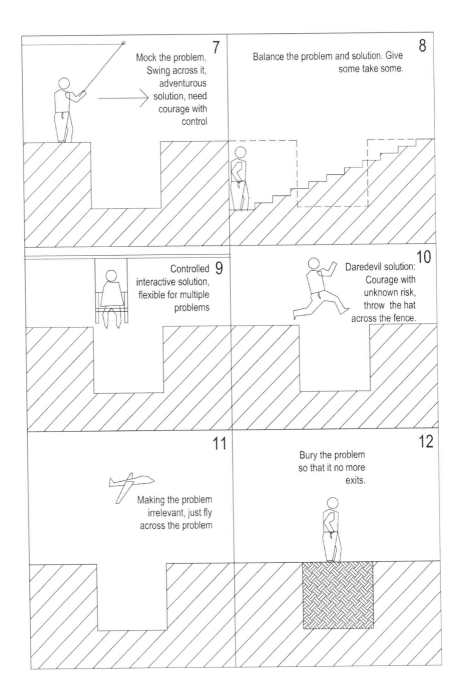

Foundation of your Solution

The example of the trench shows us that the foundation of any solution to any problem or situation lies within us because the essential characteristics within us drive us to a particular solution.

When you come across a problem, what is the thought process that follows your mind? Do you walk away from the problem? Do you decide to face it yourself? Do you think there could be more than one solution to the problem you are facing? Where you thinking at infinity and planning at 1:100?

The trench example is provided to assist you as a reference sketch to be used as a tool by which you can visualize any problem (comparing it to a trench) in a broader analytical way and find better solutions. It can be used as a symbol of your solution.

My discussions and analysis with Ashsih, Rakesh and Rohit on perceptions, scales, and characteristics had by now established within ourselves that 'to truly be successful we need to think in alignment of principles of infinity, which will give us much more meaningful solutions in our lives'. And that to achieve anything we will need to plan at all scales and deliver at 1:100, the way people understand it.

MANAGING THOUGHT PROCESS

To plan in all scales would not be an easy task; all of us knew that. We wanted to figure out a way, how best we can manage so many things at one time. As we believed the leaders had enormous talent or highly motivated they may have achieved this by some way or the other. As we scratched our heads to find the best way to plan ahead, one station passed another but we could really not think of anything which could help us plan in so many scales and yet remain focused on our aim, and suddenly our eyes fell on one advertisement it read "MBA in Six Months"

Chart the Path

So how do you really achieve anything in today's modern age? What are the concepts of today, so to say, the language of explaining ideas to people, how to think and how to work at their own scale? In the good old days the people believed more in religion, god, myths, believed in belief in people. I don't say these have vanished from the planet but people in today's age are a different breed of generations, they believe in quick fix and do not have time for a long term outlook. And this plague of thought is not restricted to people alone it is prevalent in organizations and has become a universal phenomenon. So how does one adopt to the concepts of infinite thinking in today's fast paced life? Luckily for everyone we have something used extensively in our day to day life, in our office and world over. It's called "Management".

By using the principles of management we can chart our paths in a clear yet concise way to move ahead towards our goals. There are infinite numbers of books rolled out each year talking about the principles of management. Here is a list of the basic principles followed in all managerial practices along with the infinite thinking as a basis of working out solutions.

- Have a Vision = Objective + Infinite Thinking = infinite payback of success and happiness.
- Defined Objective: Example "Designing a car"
- Infinite thinking : Example "car will help in improving air quality"
- Make Objective specific, measurable, achievable, relevant and within timelines.
- Try to sub divided the objective into smaller packages, divided objectives into smaller manageable objectives, in management jargon work breakdown structure.
- The wbs will help in planning your resources and time scheduling.

You can then set milestones, priorities which thing needs to be done first, meet the milestones and move closer to your goal.

But often everything does not go according to plan and you have to chart your plan again. It could be because of many reasons but still you have to replan your strategy to meet your final goal. So we have to not only chart the plan but be ready to chart the plan again and again if required to achieve our goals.

"There is no one way to success, infact success just happens to come on the way to something much higher"

Change the Path

Once you have charted the path and move on the charted path you are bound to get the fruits and failures of that path all along and it will test all your characteristics mentioned in the prerequisites before. This is the real test of every person thinking on the path of infinity. The great leaders see these obstacles as challenges and hurdles which have to be crossed, just like the examples we discussed a few chapters back, each obstacle is seen as a mini goal in itself with the solution taken from the principles of infinity, but what they do best is that they do not change their goal, they may change the path to achieve the same but their goal remains intact. Their strategy changes, plans change, because they know change is constant but they remain firm of their goals. This is the most important aspect of going for the goal, believing that there are different ways/ paths of achieving your goal and if you maintain the principles of infinity and characters that last, there will be no turning back. Here again I would like to mention the science of management will help you to be systematic in your approach to change, by introducing the science of change management you will be in better shape to plan the change, but it will help only when you truly imbibe the prerequisites mentioned earlier, as change is something which usually gives most of the people surprise at first, that may throw most of the people off track from your goal. It could be death in your house, job loss, divorce, child birth, mental trauma, betrayal, financial instability, winning a lottery, getting a raise or anything else. People who overcome these incidences generally tend to achieve their goals, people who don't, tend to take some other path where someone else leads them to.

Most of us in our day to day life do manage to change or adapt to change by convincing ourselves to the change in some way or the other.

One Journey Ends New Journey Begins

When I had first met Rohit I had come to know that he had changed his job for better work profile and better pay, but that also meant that he would have to travel 30km extra by his car than he used to travel earlier. This also meant that he would need to drive more, spend more, leave much early because of traffic in Mumbai. But he had then decided to change his mode of transport. He believed that traveling by train is better than traveling by car as the latter pollutes the environment. He could have easily said no to that job saying oh man it is on the other side of the town from where he stays. He now seems to be very happy with his decision.

In a way Rohit had used the concepts of plan @ 1:100 and think at 1: infinity to his own good, still he was contributing to the society at large, he was an excellent example to prove to colleagues that if you follow principles of infinite thinking you not only do good to yourself but also to humanity without stretching yourself out of the way.

I need not convince Rohit anymore. He convinced all of us through his own example of blood donation and environment friendly attitude that planning at 1:100 and thinking at infinity has its multiple benefits some tangible others intangible. By serving yourself in a particular way you can serve others as well and in turn enjoy the benefits for a longer period of time.

I had won the challenge hands down, Ashish, Rohit and Rakesh, by their own admission believed in the concepts of infinite thinking. They believed that legends did plan at 1:100 and thought at 1: infinity and that as long as we don't, we will remain to be commoners of our society.

I wanted to call Watson and tell him to drive down to the nearest eatery to show him my new laptop!

Through our journey we had learnt that by using the method of "The Wall" and "The Trench" it was very easy to face, understand and solve the many problems we face in our personal and professional lives and by aligning our thought process to principles of infinity get better solutions to our problems. It was like a new journey altogether.

As I continued through my new journey aware of the concepts of plan at 1:100 and think at 1: infinity and implementing it in my everyday life I noticed that I hardly saw Ashish, Rohit and Rakesh. We do spend time together but definitely much lesser than ever before. Sometimes I even wonder if they were real people or just people in my mind.

After I had read different books on Inspiration, Motivation and Change management I realized, that, If you do not change you can become 'Extinct' and after my journey in the local trains of Mumbai I came to know that if you Plan at 1:100 and Think at 1: Infinity you become 'Immortal'.

"Your beliefs become your thoughts. Your thoughts become your words. Your words become become your actions. Your actions become your habits. Your habits become your values. Your values become your destiny."—Mahatma Gandhi

SECTION THREE

GO BEYOND

Spirit of Humanity

SPIRIT OF HUMANITY

You may ask why, do you need to align your thoughts to these principles when you can just become successful in life by doing hard work?

You are absolutely correct in your argument when you would say that. Yes! You can be a successful person by doing just hard work and you may live a highly successful life in terms of health, wealth and prosperity. And you may close your eyes to all the problems the world is going through, thinking you will not be affected by it. If you are lucky, you may really not be affected by it at all. But the same definitely cannot be said about your next generation, can you? Because with you, dies your perceptions. You can be a big fish in a small pond, but to live in the ocean of infinity you have to think in terms of waves of ocean. The spirit of humanity is the only thing which really separates us from the animals. Let us ask ourselves an honest question, do we as Humans, Organizations and Governments really get affected, if we don't follow the principles of infinity?

WHY WE SHOULD THINK AT INFINITY

Since we develop our perceptions from the day we are born, we are the creators of our seeds we sow, In other words, we reap what we sow. If that is the case, then whatever problems we are facing today isn't it the consequence of what we have done before? Think about it. The problems we are facing externally may have been because of someone else, but we are equally responsible for it. We can't blame the municipal authorities for clogged drains if we are using plastic bags for our groceries and throwing it in the gutters! The cat drinking the milk closing her eyes cannot shy away from the consequences it will face for drinking the milk. We can't close our eyes to it. Have you ever stopped a man from spitting in public places? Did you ever think of buying a house where there was a lush green forest few years ago and it made way for your dream home?

There are of course many reasons for thinking at Infinity at a personal and professional level; but won't it be a wonderful thing for you to know, that, what you do at your level does make a difference in the world to make it a better place to live in?

WHY CORPORATE SHOULD THINK AT INFINITY

Corporate Houses work on Human Resource, their success or failure depends on how well their resource functions and carries outs its duties. How its image is seen by its clients and customers depends on the employee who works with them. If it imbibes the spirit of humanity within its culture it will get better performance and productivity from its employees. Its client will have trust in its function and ability. The principles of infinite thinking can imbibe an ethical way of working in the organization ensuring protection and growth of company assets.

Would there be a company which wouldn't want to touch each and every human being in the world?

WHY THE GOVERNMENT/ WORLD SHOULD THINK AT INFINITY

Some problems are easy to solve and can take few seconds to solve. Some are more complex and take much more time. The problems the world faces today are terrorism, corruption, dieses, poverty, racial discrimination, gender bias, illiteracy, the list seems endless and they are much more complex and beyond the calculations of human genius. They can really be solved with the thought of infinite thinking. The principles of infinite thinking go beyond the time barrier. Since the principle themselves have stood the test of time, adhering to it will ensure that the solution stands the test of time.

Globally many countries are suffering at the hands of terrorism. In spite of the best efforts from many countries terrorism survives on global level, how can it be stopped? Poverty and disease are still a part of our daily life. We see and hear about many people die of starvation, what are we doing about it? Our natural resources are getting depleted day by day what are we doing about it? In India there are so many children uneducated, what is the solution for such a problem? The world is going through financial crisis what can be done about it?

Talking about global problems, are we really successful if we see so many problem staring on our face? Isn't it time to stand up and do something about it?

Would there be any nation in this world which does not want World Peace?

THE DEATH OF SPIRIT OF HUMANITY

3 blast rocked Mumbai in 2011, news poured in about what happened, where it happened and what can be done and what should have been done. Home ministry had started issuing statements every two hours about the update on situation. People were angry and upset over the police, politicians and every other person who were supposed to be 'responsible' for their safety and security in the first place. Somehow unfortunately I started finding similar patterns of overtones of individuals in crisis, people complaint, politician's promises, and police conducts road blocks and through sheer hard work and intelligence manage to pin point the culprits who did this unforgettable action. It takes quiet some time, effort and money to get this whole process going and completed. Sometimes even the best efforts yield no result and the case remains unsolved. I briefly went through the news channels and interviews of people and I heard them say politicians are useless, police arrives late, there was not enough help, our security is compromised, and the complaints were endless. I wanted to agree and join the chorus; but somewhere I felt there has to be a better way. Blaming others could be the best way to wash our hands free of it. This enables us to continue to live our normal life and let the others take the blame for it. Let's for once imagine that the nation (world) is your home, you are but a part of the family, the way you take care of your house, whether you are the youngest or elder most you are equally responsible for the betterment of the house. Your politicians, police personal are all but part of your family, they have been assigned a role to play, they may have failed from your perspective but imagine this from the perspective of a person leaving in an unstable hostile country, they would be wanting to come to India, as they would believe India is a safer place than their own country.

My question is, will catching or killing law breakers really solve the problems if they are deep rooted? Today's problems need to be tackled at grass root levels. We have to begin all over again, we may not be able to see the change, but this step today will ensure a better world for tomorrow. We should act now to resolve our problems that have been plaguing us since so long, we are now on the verge of a virtual collapse in terms of natural resources, human values and in essence the spirit of humanity somehow seems to be at stake. But how do we tackle such great issues? We the common men of our times, what powers do we really have to make a difference to this world. How can individuals like us fight terrorism, poverty, disease, natural disaster which even mighty nations of the world find it difficult to tackle?

The answer lies in the spirit of this book we have to Plan @ 1:100 and Think @ 1:∞. Go deep inside this very thought process and you will see what the Legends saw, they saw a better place to live in, a better tomorrow. I see it, I believe in it. If every one of us does, it can take on anything in this world, think about it.

The death of spirit of humanity can be avoided if all of us think, act and go beyond our personal happiness, which to me is the essence of being immortal.

GOING BEYOND

From my perspective there has to be a twofold strategy to keep the Spirit of Humanity alive.

- Imbibe the qualities and principles of infinity into people of this generation, educate them, and motivate them to do better in their everyday life.
- Imbibe the qualities and principles of infinity into the next following generations to make them into people who will form the foundation of a better tomorrow. And maintain the process.

To change our thought process once we grow up is a very challenging task. Since people tend to live in their own perception and are stubborn about it, imbibing the principles of infinite thinking can be quiet challenging, but we have to try and adapt to this philosophy if we want to see a positive change in ourselves and our world. Once we are convinced about it we also need to promote the spirit of Humanity amongst our fellow citizens, this would require lot of patients and tolerance on our part. But still this is just a small problem; if all the nations think infinitely, it may well be a cake walk.

At grass root levels there can be many ways to promote the spirit of humanity in our neighboring communities, we can,

1. Make it compulsory to print the principles of humanity in local news paper.
2. Radio message it, hearing makes the information go to heart and information heard somehow tends to last longer in the memory for some people.
3. Send motivational message through local trains, bus and public transport.
4. Make the spirit of humanity philosophy a compulsion in schools and colleges.

There should be no political or religious overtones to these messages. These will make people more confident, they will develop positive attitude and in general there will be an increase in the productivity of the country. This will help everyone personally, professionally and socially.

The step two to attaining the goal is the one which requires each one of us to imbibe the spirit of humanity in the next generation. In step two, we have to nurture the next generation on the principles of Infinity. This would be the longest and the most challenging step towards achieving the goal. It may mean several challenges and this book is too small to collate all possible challenges and changes this two step philosophy will take, but the way I see it, I believe by taking these first two steps we can achieve success not just in our personal, professional and social lives but also bring harmony and peace in the world. This will ensure that the spirit of humanity prevails infinitely.

"**You must be the change you wish to see in the World**"—Mahatma Gandhi

ACKNOWLEDGEMENTS

To my brother Vivek Deshmukh for reacting in a very challenging way initially and then helping me throughout this process of writing the book and bringing it to this level.

He has been an invaluable guide for this successful journey.

I would also like to thank all the authors of the self help books for writing such wonderful books and inspiring me to write this book

A special Thanks to the Lord for giving The Bhagavad Gita.

BIBLIOGRAPHY

The Bhagavad Gita

Road Signs for Success by Jim Whitt

The Seven Habits of Highly Effective People by Stephen R. Covey

All I really need to know I learned in Kindergarten by Robert Fulghum

Rich Dada Poor Dad by Robert T. Kiyosaki

The Secret by Rhonda Byrne

Successful Project Management by Ken Lawson

Who Moved my Cheese by Dr. Spencer Johnson

Finding a Purpose in Life by R. M. Lala

What got you here won't get you there by Marshall Goldsmith

The Song of God by Kirtanananda Swami Bhaktipada

Finding Strength in Difficult Times by David Viscott

Tactics by Edward De Bono

Project Management Secrets by Matthew Batchelor

Successful Negotiating by Ken Lawson

How to Enjoy your Life and your Job by Dale Carnegie

The 100 Simple Secrets of Happy Family by David Niven

I'm Ok You're Ok by Thomas A. Harris

The Alchemist by Paulo Coelho

Awaken the Giant Within by Anthony Robbins

The Magic of Thinking Big by David J. Schwartz